Rothley

Then and Now

A century of change seen through the

CAMERA LENS

Published by Rothley History Society

© 2003
2nd Edition 2006

Rothley History Society

Designed and typeset by: Ron Billings, Rearsby

Printed by: Scotia Press, Leicester

ISBN No: 0-9545426-0-6

Front cover: Cottages that once stood on Woodgate near the village centre. Photographed c1910.

Rear cover: These cottages, still standing, were erected by Harry Hames in 1929 to replace those on the front cover.

PREFACE

MORE accomplished historians than ourselves have published books on the history of Rothley that range from personal reminiscences to detailed exploration of specific aspects of village life and for the serious student they are essential reading. This book hopes to complement this scholarship by presenting a more general pictorial view of the changes to the village during the last hundred years.

"Rothley – Then and Now" had its inception at the end of the last century when the Rothley History Society held its inaugural meeting. The newly formed committee studied proposals for a Millennium project such as a calendar or a leaflet in the form of a 'Historical Trail' around the village. After much discussion the result is this book which was born out of a desire to show the village as it used to be, how it looks today and to provide a reference point, for those who follow us, to the further changes that will inevitably take place in the years to come.

The village has changed enormously during the last fifty years, and anyone coming to settle here today can have little idea of how different it looked before World War II. It was once a village where most residents earned their living by manual labour, hosiery, boot and shoe making, the granite quarry at Mountsorrel, farming and, not many years earlier, domestic service. The industrial base has now almost disappeared, surviving only as a few service industries on several sites in Fowke Street.

The layout we have adopted contrasts, in most instances, each picture of the past with a current image on the opposite page. After a look at two aspects of our ancient history mentioned in the introduction the picture sequence on the subsequent pages is arranged as if one is entering the village from the old A6 (once the Turnpike) via Hallfields Lane and up North Street to Cross Green. From there we explore in turn the streets that lead from Cross Green and then proceed to other streets in Rothley. After this topographical tour we look at transport and how it has changed then at some of the notable characters of the past, some of whom have left an indelible mark on the village. Towards the end there are other pictures which are included either because we liked them or because they show that sometimes things do not change very much after all.

We hope that this book will recall memories for those who read it, wherever they are now, who may have lived through much of the change pictured here. We also hope it will provide a glimpse into the past and a guide around our village for its children, for visitors and for those who come after us.

THE CHANGING NAME OF ROTHLEY

THE name Rothley is derived from the Old English roth (a clearing) and leah (glade, clearing, meadow) and the following are some of the variations, with the exception of the last, which were found on a list in the County Record Office. The sources were not given but they presumably appeared on documents bearing the dates given.

1086	RODELEI
1154	ROTHELEA
1217	ROLLAY
1284	ROTHELEYE
1348	ROTELEI
1558	ROTHELY
1572	ROTHLIE
1641	ROTHELEY
1671	ROATHLEY

Until the first dictionaries were published during the 18th century spelling was at the whim of the writer and generally phonetic. This would account for some of the variations above, particularly those which are quite close in date. The first on the list is as it appears in the Domesday Book and the last one is significant in that it appears to confirm the local use today of the long 'o' (as in code). People from further afield tend to pronounce Rothley with a short 'o' (as in hot). The last variation (Roathley) leaves little doubt as to the intended pronunciation. It appears in the manuscript 'The Recipe Book of Archdale Palmer, lord of the manor of Wanlip' (transcribed and published by the Sycamore Press in 1985), which he compiled between 1659-1672. Wanlip is only two miles from Rothley so he must have been familiar with the local pronunciation.

The use of the name in the form we are familiar with today has been recorded in one or two documents of the 17th century but, given the great variation in spelling at the time, they were most likely accidental. The name probably became permanently established in its present form during the first half of the 18th century since it appears as Rothley in the Leicestershire Quarter Sessions records for the licensing of inns in 1753.

ACKNOWLEDGEMENTS

We would like to thank:–

- The following people and organisations who have loaned pictures and given us permission to use them or allowed us to take photographs –

    Bradley's, Rothley; Mrs. M. Calloway, Birstall; Mrs. E. Chester, Birstall; The County Record Office; Mr. K. Kitching, Rothley; Leicester Mercury; Mrs. M. Offley, Rothley; Mr. T. Sheppard, Rothley; Mr. & Mrs. F. Sleath, Rothley; Mr. B. Verity, Rothley; Mr. K. Walpole; Mr. P. Warner, Rothley; Mrs. D. Wright, Rothley CE Primary School; The Wardens of the Church of St. Mary's & St. John's.

- The many people who supplied information about the history of Rothley.

- Members of the Society and others who contributed to the cost of publication and supported our fund raising activities.

- And, not least, to:

    Mr. Ron Billings for his generosity in providing his expertise for the design, layout, scanning and typesetting of this book.

Compiled and written by

Maureen Bulmer, Ann Harmer, Sue Joyce,

John Brooks, Peter Newbold

INTRODUCTION

ARCHAEOLOGICAL evidence of the history of Rothley dates back at least to Roman times and its extensive documented history started with an entry in the Domesday book and continued through its association with the Knights Templar and the Babington family.

In 1896, during the digging of the cutting for Rothley railway station, the diggers uncovered skeletons from a Saxon burial ground and, close by, mosaics from a Roman building. W. T. Tucker F.G.S. became actively interested in the discovery and gave a paper regarding the finds to the Leicester Literary & Philosophical Society. Several of these objects are now in the Jewry Wall Museum in Leicester. During the construction of the Ridgeway, in 1901, more of the villa site was exposed and Tucker again recorded whatever was unearthed. The finds included a concrete floor, wall foundations, a hypercaust (underfloor heating) and a well. From a geophysical survey carried out in 2000 by a local resident it is now estimated that the villa was of a courtyard type extending across the fields on both sides of the Ridgeway with views westward towards Charnwood Forest.

Although the Saxon burial site existed near the Roman villa there is no evidence of Saxon settlement above ground in Rothley itself apart from the monument on the South side of the church of St. Mary and St. John (see picture 1). It has long been held to be 9th century but modern scholarship is now suggesting an 11th century origin. Whatever the outcome of that debate it conforms closely in style to other Saxon crosses and is carved from millstone grit and has no crosshead. Its four weathered faces, each divided into four panels, are decorated with plants, scrolls, intricate plait work and, on the south face, a mythical winged creature. Fewer than fifty of these crosses now survive and ours is one of only two in the East Midlands. They served as community meeting points or burial markers and many were deliberately destroyed or used as building material. Rothley is fortunate to have retained such a tangible link with its past, especially one which provides a valuable 'window' on to the art styles and craftsmanship of our medieval forefathers.

The ancient manor estate of Rothley originally belonged to the Crown but in 1231 it was given to the Knights Templar by Henry III. Here they established a preceptory and a chapel (see picture 2). The Templars were disbanded in 1312 and their estates transferred to the Knights Hospitaller until they in turn were dissolved in 1540. In 1529 Humphrey Babington, brother of a Preceptor, acquired a lease on the manor and his son Thomas bought it outright in 1565. Ownership stayed with the Babingtons until 1845 when it was acquired by Sir James Parker who had married into the Babington family. When his son sold the estate in 1893 it was bought by Frederick Merttens, a businessman from Manchester.

Rothley Temple was the birthplace of Lord Macaulay and a focal point for those working for the abolition of slavery in the 19th century. The Leicestershire Record Office holds a large archive of material on these and other topics of local interest which may be consulted by those who wish to know more.

To set the scene for the pictorial review of Rothley in the following pages and to provide a flavour of what Rothley was like in the 19th century we can refer to White's Directories for the County of Leicestershire. As in most villages descendants of some of the people named still live locally.

In 1846 Rothley was 'a large and pleasant village on the banks of a rivulet' with a population of 1055 and 1230 acres of fertile land. The parish also included the southern end of Mountsorrel and several chapelries in East Goscote Hundred (an ecclesiastical division of land). Reference was made to the Barrow on Soar Union Workhouse (today's Linkfield Road was once known as Union Lane) and to the Court House on Cross Green 'an ancient building with a pyramidal roof with a nearby lock-up for wrongdoers'. Many of the villagers earned their living as framework knitters or through agriculture and the directory mentions a draper, a wheelwright, two bakers, a brewer, a corn miller, a saddler and two blacksmiths. The village had two boot and shoe makers, three butchers (William Chamberlain, Joseph Barsby and William Draycott), three grocers and two carriers (William Lovett and William North).

The vicar at the time was the Rev. Ackworth and there were chapels belonging to the Wesleyans, the Primitive Methodists (now part of the Roods development on Mountsorrel Lane and opposite the row of cottages known as 'Ranters Row') and the General Baptists. The village had a Free School, founded in 1683, when Benjamin Hickling left a cottage in Town Green Street and several pieces of land in trust for the 'education of 14 or 15 poor boys of Rothley'. Girls were not catered for until 1736 when Mrs. Eliza Daniel gave £30 in trust for a schoolmistress 'to teach poor girls to read'. Rothley Temple was described as a separate estate outside the parish. It had been sold on the death of Thomas Babington to James Parker (who had married Thomas's daughter Mary in 1829), and included 13 houses and 42 inhabitants.

By 1887 Rothley was a 'considerable township'. The church, referred to in 1846 as St. Mary's, was now St. John's (today called St. Mary's and St. John's) and had been extensively restored in 1878 by the efforts of Rev. Richard Burton at a cost of £4,000. He was also reported as being responsible for the rebuilding of the National School in School Street, contributing £500 towards the cost (see picture 43).

Industry had reached the village with the establishment of two 'boot manufactories' and the hosiery works of Tebbutt & Co. A library and reading room were operating and the Post Office had been set up 'at Henry Brewin's'. Rothley had five public houses; the Bluebell, the Old Crown, the Royal Oak, the Old Red Lion (also known as Rothley House and the only inn recorded in the 1846 edition) and the Woodman's Stroke where Edward Hickling had a brewhouse and also worked as a wheelwright.

By this time, the village had a milliner and straw hat maker, four dressmakers, several gardeners and market gardeners, a brick maker on Rothley Plain and three builders, one of whom, Frank Sleath, was also a painter. The village of the 1840s, with its framework knitters and largely agricultural employment base, had diversified and expanded to meet the needs of the late 19th century. As a footnote the population of the village was recorded in 1999 as 3,493.

1. This obelisk, referred to on all maps as the Saxon Cross, stands on the south side of the church. Long held to be 9th century, hence its label Saxon, more recent scholarship now suggests that it may date from about 200 years later and have Viking connections. We suspect that this is a debate which will rumble on for some long time to come but what cannot be in dispute is that we are fortunate to have this well preserved ancient relic in our midst as a reminder of the long history of the occupation of our village.

2. We are fortunate that Rothley has a well documented history since 1231 thanks largely to its long association with the Knights Templar, the Knights Hospitaller and their successors the Babington family, all of whom occupied Rothley Temple. The chapel, on the right, is regarded as the finest surviving Templar chapel outside London. The Temple estate, although part of the village, existed independently of the parish for administrative purposes until the late 19th century.

1a. We obviously cannot contrast the cross, as it once looked, with what we see today. This picture, therefore, shows its relationship to the church, to the left of the birch tree centre foreground, and half hidden among the trees.

2a. Rothley Temple has now become Rothley Court Hotel and this is the first view one has of it on driving past the lodge gates. Apart from the addition of a porch entrance the frontage has changed very little since the 18th century. The Templars' chapel is to the right and on the lawn to the left of the lamp post a small monument reminds us that William Wilberforce drafted the bill to abolish slavery at Rothley Temple.
The bill was passed in 1833.

THE CHANGING SHAPE OF ROTHLEY

3. The old A6 looking north showing Lazenby's garage and the Red Lion in the 1960s.
The A6, once known as the Turnpike, has now been replaced by a by-pass. Earlier owners, in the 1930s, also ran a roller skating rink in a building behind the garage.

4. The Red Lion in the early years of the 20th century. It had once been a coaching inn known as Rothley House; the name which still appears on the walls in this picture. Not many years earlier the 1891 census showed 9 people living there – Arthur Satchell, the landlord and also a farmer, his wife and daughter, his mother-in-law, a barmaid, a general servant, a groom, an ostler and a 'boots'. They presumably had a lot of passing carriage trade.

3a. The A6 and the Red Lion today. The garage and the house on the corner were cleared about 1980 and the garage was rebuilt further back on the site. Today the garage has gone and the building is used by the County Library Service. A by-pass (out of sight to the right) means that the old carriage route now carries only local traffic.

4a. The Red Lion in 2003 looking smart after its latest refit. For many years after WW II it was run by the Dimblebee family. The low buildings to the right were once outbuildings and stables but now house the restaurant and children's play area.

5. The bridge on Hallfields Lane known as Nott Bridge. It was extremely narrow and the wide verges, still surviving on either side, are evidence of access to the fords on each side of the bridge which were once used by farm carts and other heavy transport.

6. North Street looking north. When this picture was taken there was a continuous frontage as far as the Old Crown inn on the left. The end of 'Dutchman's wall' can be seen on the right.

5a. The present bridge on Hallfields Lane was erected about 1935. Hallfields Lane appeared on maps as Rothley House Lane until quite recently. A few houses, between the east end of the bridge and the entrance to the allotments, were built between 1903 and 1929. All other development up to the Red Lion has taken place since then.

6a. North Street today. There is now a gap in the frontage to the left, where a building has disappeared, which is the car park of the Old Crown Inn. Three houses, built in the 1990s, occupy the site on the right.

7. The east side of North Street looking north. This view shows North St. before 1901 when Sleath & Son replaced the old cottages to the right and built the terraced houses which replace part of the stone wall beyond them. The tall cottage in the middle distance survives.

8. The top end of North Street on the corner of Woodgate. These are very old houses which were demolished about 1953/4. The tall chimney was known locally as 'the lighthouse'.

7a. East side of North St. looking north today. The two cottages were built by Sleath in 1901. The surviving part of the wall, seen opposite, flanks the car park behind the Royal Oak. A good stretch of the old raised pavement still survives. This was quite a common feature in Rothley. See the picture of Fowke Street (picture 18).

8a. The top end of North Street today showing the entrance to the Baptist Chapel. The original entrance was on Woodgate and the present entrance was built when the houses in the picture opposite were removed.

9. Woodgate from Cross Green showing the same house on the corner of North Street that appears in picture 8 but now rendered white. The houses on the right of Woodgate, in the distance, have been replaced by a block of four maisonettes.

10. Cross Green looking towards North Street with the court house on the left. This was taken before the erection of the War Memorial in 1921 and Cross Green appears as an open space. The court house was where the Lord of the Manor sat twice a year to hear and settle local disputes and collect fees and rents due. He was also entitled to collect a commission on any land or property sales made by non-residents of the village. In later years the court house was used to store the local fire engine.

9a. The view opposite as it appears today. The dominant feature is the entrance to the Baptist Chapel. The shop on the corner to the right, currently the 'Mercury' shop, was for many years Goodall's grocers and later Grange Dairy.

10a. Cross Green looking towards North Street. The bus shelter is on the left. The building marked Bass & Co on the right of the opposite picture had gone long before the new town houses were recently built. The rose bed in the corner of Cross Green by the bus shelter marks the site of the court house. The white building to the left is The Royal Oak Inn.

11. A view across Cross Green looking from the entrance to Woodgate. The Court House has gone, as has the stone 'lock-up' which once stood at the Mountsorrel Lane end of the green. This picture was presumably taken not long before the War Memorial was installed. Note the cottages with thatched roofs between the trees (See picture 14).

We have given prominence to the pictures on these two pages and those on pages 40 and 41 because Rothley is unusual in having two village greens. One of them must have been the site of the weekly market and annual fair that were held, for only a short period, by rights granted in 1285.

11a. Cross Green from Woodgate today.

These are presumably the same trees which appear in the picture opposite. The thatched cottages have now gone. The area around Cross Green is due to be remodelled in March 2003 so this view is also about to become history.

12. Cross Green looking towards Fowke Street. The Royal Oak is on the right. This view, with everybody turned out in their best clothes, was taken on a Bank Holiday. The year was 1917 or earlier since the message on the card is dated August 1917. The building to the left of the Royal Oak, once a sweet shop run by Mr. & Mrs. Elkington, has been replaced by the entrance to the car park. The building in the centre distance, on the corner of Anthony Street and Fowke Street, was originally the Co-op.

13. This cruck cottage in Church Street is one of several in Rothley that are still occupied today although their original 15/16th century owners would certainly not recognise the interiors. The 'crucks' are 'A' frames of tree trunks, often visible at the ends of the building, serving as the supports around which the dwelling was built. In 1954 there were ten cruck houses in Rothley but several have since disappeared. The theory has been advanced that Rothley is rich in this type of construction because it remained a poor working class village until comparatively recent times and the owners could not afford to rebuild in more modern styles. Whatever the reason these houses endow Rothley with some of the character it possesses today. The bronze gate is one of the memorial gates to Catherine Broadhurst at the entrance to the churchyard. Howard Broadhurst succeeded Frederick Merttens as the owner of Rothley Temple.

12a. The current view of Cross Green to Fowke Street. The end cottage on the east side of Cross Green where it joins Fowke Street, visible in the opposite photo, has disappeared and is replaced by a small garden. When the whole area is remodelled the stretch of road straight ahead will be closed at the near end to provide more car parking space and to improve pedestrian safety.

13a. Today's residents in Rothley demand a very much higher standard of comfort than was ever available in cruck cottages of the past. To highlight modern aspirations The Roods is an award winning development of town houses in the centre of the village built on the industrial site of the old Star Works. Compare these with the cottages built by Sleath & Son one hundred years ago and speculate on what building in Rothley will look like 100 years from today.

14. East side of Cross Green in 1910 looking towards Anthony Street. The thatched cottages were bought by Rev. R. Burton in 1878 for £1,233 - 18s - 0d. In the 1960s they were demolished to provide an access road to Greenway Close.

15. Dedication of the War Memorial on Cross Green 4/7/21. According to Ruth Packe in her history of Rothley (1958) it was supplied and erected free of charge by the Mountsorrel Granite Company but she remarks that "the specifications given to them by the Memorial Committee were not carried out". She continues, "when erected the memorial was somewhat of a disappointment".

14a. The entrance to Greenway Close which now replaces the site of the cottages in picture 14. The building on the left, now Corts hardware store, was originally built and occupied by Barclays Bank. How the bank got planning permission to erect a building whose style was at such odds with the appearance of the rest of Cross Green must be a matter for regret.

15a. The War Memorial today. Originally there were railings immediately round the memorial while the rest of Cross Green was unfenced. Total enclosure came later.

16. House in Anthony Street, before modernisation, that once belonged to Draycott the butchers. They were also land owners and local benefactors.
The gabled extension to the street was the butcher's shop and they had their own slaughterhouse on the site.

17. Houses on the west side of Anthony Street at its junction with Cross Green. These houses, as far as the gable end at right angles to the street, were demolished about 1931. The steps outside the first cottage were apparently know as the 'gossiping' steps.

16a. The lower half of Anthony Street looking towards The Woodman's Stroke. The house on the right is the one in the opposite picture with what was the butcher's shop now incorporated into the main house. The house on the left also, at one time, belonged to a member of the Draycott family.

17a. Current view of the location on the opposite page. Note the house in the background in both pictures with a tall chimney and its gable end to the street. It survives today and is one of the oldest houses in Rothley.

18. Fowke Street in 1909. The house in the right foreground burnt down in the 1950s. The cottage beyond the children on the left now has the date 1727 picked out across its front wall.

19. This photograph was presumably taken at the time of the construction of the building which today serves as the village Hall in Fowke Street. It was the gift of Harry Hames to the village. If the date stone now set in the frontage, but not apparent in this picture, is reliable it was originally built as the Reading Room since that is how it is described on the map of 1903.

18a. Fowke Street today. The left side has changed very little. But the old house on the right which burnt down was replaced by the present modern house which stands well above street level. This house and another beyond the white cottage demonstrate the disregard for the aesthetic appearance of the street shown by planning authorities prior to the 1970s.

19a. The Village Hall today. The frontage is little changed but an entrance annexe has been added at the left and it has been extended at the rear. The date stones for 1886 are visible on either side of the central window. It is not clear when it changed its use from Reading Room to Village Hall.

20. Mountsorrel Lane looking north. The left side of this view starts at the Rothley Centre which at the time of this picture was the Liberal Club. The first stage of Woodfield Road, built by F. Sleath & Son before WW II, leads from the end of the houses on the left. There were very few houses further along after that.

21. Mountsorrel Lane looking towards Cross Green.

20a. Mountsorrel Lane today. The foreground has changed little but buildings now extend along the whole length of Mountsorrel Lane. The school is on the right beyond the 20 MPH signs which were designed by the school children as part of the recently installed traffic calming measures. The Rothley Centre, on the left, started life in 1911 as the Liberal Club and was converted for community use in 1980. It also houses the Parish Council office.

21a. Mountsorrel Lane today from the same viewpoint as the picture opposite. The terrace on the left has not changed dramatically but the large tree on the right obscures the development which has taken place since the earlier photo.

22. Woodgate looking east towards Cross Green from about the junction with Howe Lane. There appear to be private dwellings between the shops on the south side. The shop front to the right was that of Burnsall the baker later taken over by Harry Chamberlain.
The other shops in that terrace were the drapery shop run by Wells and Cook the butcher.
The houses just visible on the left with steps up to the front doors have been replaced by a block of four maisonettes.

23. Woodgate looking west from the Baptist Chapel. The house on the extreme right had a shop front added in the 1960s when it opened as a hardware store. Next to the last awning on the right was a stile giving access to a footpath which led to The Ridings.

22a. Woodgate looking west. The same row of buildings as shown on the opposite page but taken from the other end. The travel agent is where the two bay windows were at the end of the row in the other picture.

23a. The building housing the post office and pharmacy was built in 1932 after the demolition of the house behind the lady standing on the pavement in picture 23.

24. Woodgate looking west. The large house standing well forward of the building line on the left was on the corner of Howe Lane and is now replaced by the Babington Court sheltered housing for the elderly. The houses opposite were replaced by the three cottages built by Harry Hames in 1929 and later, in the 1950s, by the entrance to Babington road.

25. A view taken in 1910 of thatched cottages set back from the road on the north side of Woodgate. They are out of sight in the picture above but the end of the wall fronting them can be seen. The other houses fronting the street have all disappeared. This is another view of the cottages on the front cover.

24a. Woodgate looking west today with the entrance to Babington Road showing the dramatic change which has taken place in this part of Rothley. The development of Babington and Macaulay roads and the extension of Woodfield Road took place in the 1950s and was the first major development in Rothley after the war.

25a. Three cottages built by Harry Hames in 1929 for his employees. They replaced the cottages illustrated on the facing page. Hames, who owned the hosiery factory known as Victoria Mills in Fowke Street, was another of Rothley's benefactors. He endowed playing fields on Mountsorrel Lane and built the Village Hall (picture 19).

26. Hyman's garage on the south side of Woodgate. When demolished in 2000 it had been much altered and sported an asbestos sheet roof but the granite walls suggested a much earlier building.

27. Cottages at the bottom of Wellsic Lane. The corner of the Bluebell Inn is just visible on the left. These cottages were at one time the premises of Fearn's the carriers. Their sign can be seen on the wall. By the 1950s they had become derelict and the local inhabitants pressed for their demolition.

26a. The house which now occupies the site of Hyman's garage on Woodgate. This is one development that could be considered as an improvement on what it replaced.

27a. New houses at the bottom of Wellsic Lane. The Bluebell Inn is on the left. It is probable that many of the cottages which were so casually replaced up to the 1970s would today be listed buildings had they survived. Aesthetic considerations in planning arrived too late to save them.

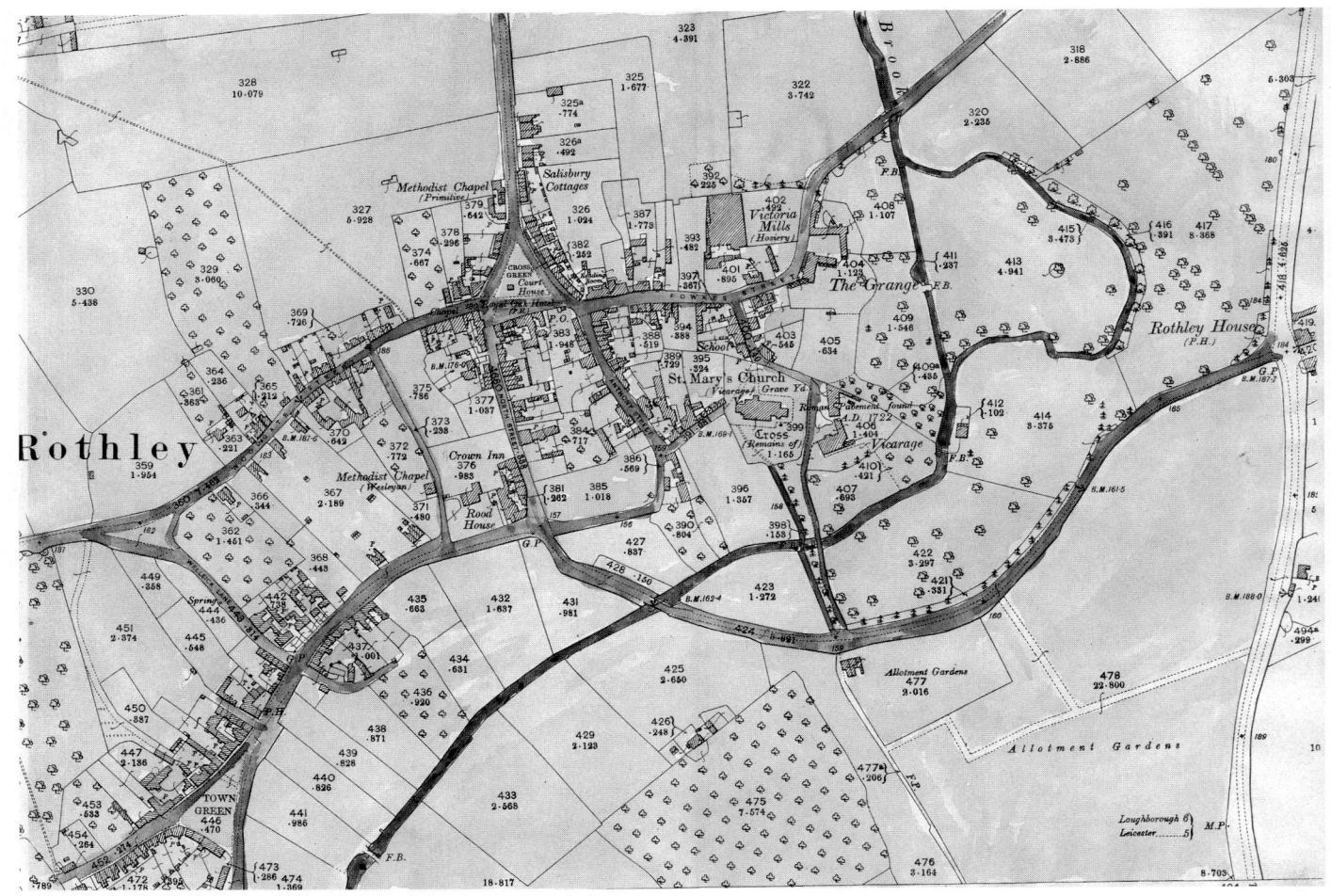

28. Rothley in 1903 before so much of the change began. The plots showing diagonal lines of trees were orchards and the Court House was still standing. The Methodist Chapel on Mountsorrel Lane is now a private dwelling and part of The Roods development. Although there was a lot more open space in the village many of the cottages presumably had little land since there was a need for allotments (bottom right). The land on which they stand is likely to be the site of the next major development in Rothley and the allotments have been moved along the old A6 towards Birstall. The school was still in School Street and the site of the Village Hall in Fowke Street was then the Reading Room. Of the public buildings only the public houses seem to have largely survived the changes of the 20th century.

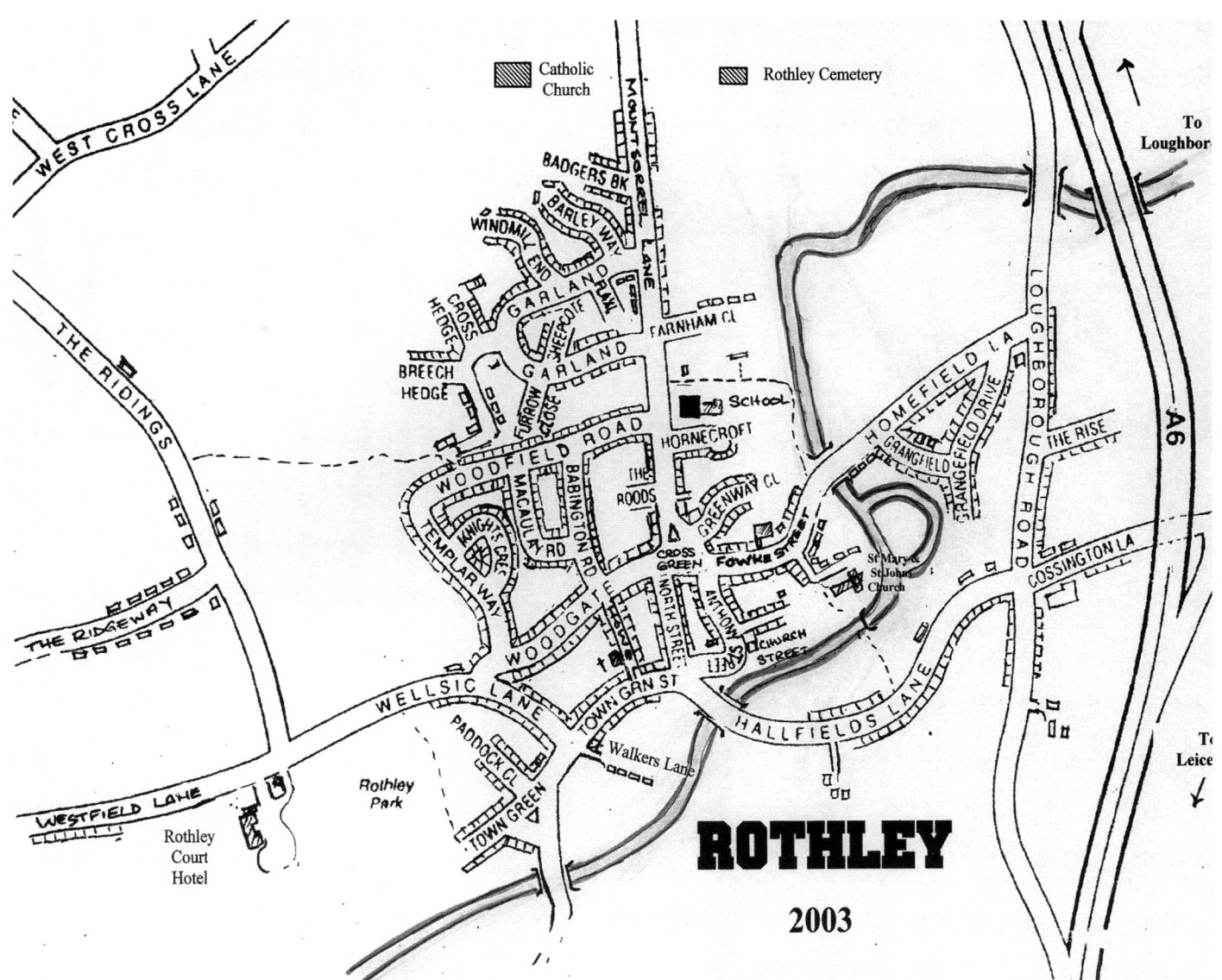

28a. Rothley today. The cross-hatched areas lining the streets on this schematic map represent buildings and, if compared with the map opposite, show the enormous amount of development and infill that has taken place in Rothley since 1903. Most of it has occurred since WW II and the building continues today.

29. Town Green Street with a group of factory hands who worked at Willetts boot & shoe factory in the alley which is now called Paddock Close.
Note that the female employees are assembled apart from the men. When this was taken, about 1920, Town Green was called Uptown.
The Bluebell Inn is on the extreme right.

30. The alley referred to in the picture above remained in industrial use until the 1990s when Brookman's woodworking machinery factory was demolished. Although not very old, this picture highlights the disappearance of industry in Rothley and the conversion of factory sites to residential use. The back of the Bluebell Inn is to the right.

29a. Town Green Street today. The factories have gone and the old doorway on the corner of the Bluebell Inn is now filled in. The firm of W. Sharpe named in the opposite photo was shown in Kelly's Directory for 1904 as Maltsters, Farmers and Coal Merchants. By 1912 they are shown only as Maltsters.

30a. Paddock Close was once known locally as Bluebell Alley. Today's view of the 'mews' type development that has replaced the factories illustrates the changes in attitudes towards planning during the last 20 years that have introduced new building to the village in a way that enhances its character.

31. This old photograph of Town Green, the oldest part of the village, still has several 15/16th century 'cruck' cottages. It retains its character and has suffered less than other parts of the village from the hands of the developer. The dirt road in the foreground once led to the ford and stepping stones (see picture 32) but now gives access to the golf course. Note the open aspect of the whole area.

31a. Town Green today. As with most of the open areas and public parts of the village Town Green now has a controlled and managed appearance. Kerb stones make such a difference! The older photographs generally display a much more casual approach to the appearance of public areas which probably reflected the priorities of the Parish Councils of the past.

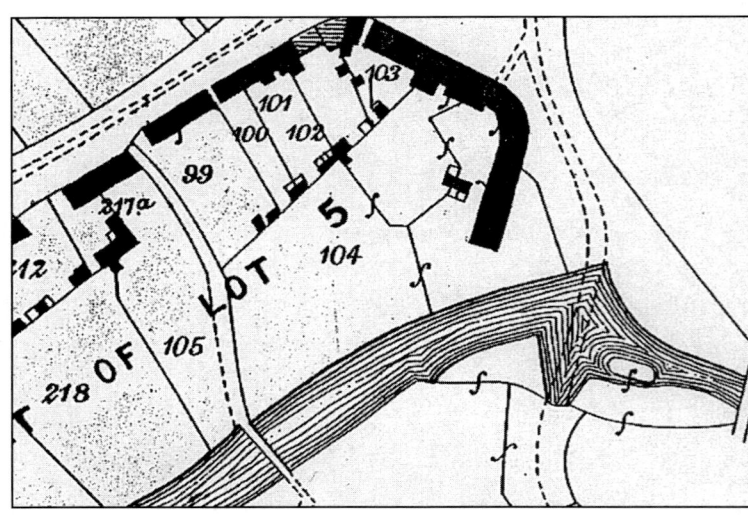

32. Stepping stones over the brook between Town Green and what is now the golf course. The roadway on the right still leads past Town Green to the Bluebell Inn and Town Green Street. This picture apparently pre-dates the building of the bridge in 1896 that replaced the footbridges on either side of the ford which can be seen on the Rothley Temple estate map of 1893.

32a. The bridge leading from Town Green to the golf course. In 1895 the owner of Rothley Temple, Frederick Merttens, applied to replace the ford with a bridge at this site. He had plans to develop part of the estate, which he had recently bought, as a Garden Suburb and one of his promotional schemes was to build the golf course which opened in 1911 and occupies the land on the far side of the bridge.

32b. This stone built bridge crosses the brook against Rothley Court Hotel. It does not appear on an estate map of 1729 but it must have been built during the 18th century since it carries a stone indicating that it was restored in 1819.

33. Town Green Street, looking west, in the 1930s. At that time it was called Main Street. The cottages in the distance are at the bottom of Wellsic Lane (see picture 27). There were two shops selling general groceries on this side and another on the opposite side. It is surprising how many people made a living running small shops. We know of at least eight scattered around the village other than those in Woodgate.

34. The lower part of Wellsic Lane during the floods of 21/22 May 1932. Flooding of Rothley Brook was a regular occurrence but that of 1932 was one of the worst in living memory when almost two inches of rain fell in 24 hours. On the 24th at a Parish Council meeting Mr. Boyer complained that the arches of Farnham bridge (on the A6) had been blocked for months but nothing had been done to clear them. Because of this the water was 4 feet higher on the village side than on the river side. Furniture was swept away and carried for miles and scores of poultry were drowned.

33a. Town Green St. today. Shops have gone as have several of the cottages to make way for the garage which is set back in the opening in the middle distance. The garage stands on the site of the first school in Rothley which was endowed by Bartholomew Hickling in 1683.

34a. Part of the flood barrier in the 'donkey' field on the west side of Hallfields Lane that has reduced flooding dramatically. This flood defence was installed from the golf course to the Woodman's Stroke during 1978-9. Since then the rare instances of minor flooding have been due to surface water backing up and not being able to run off into the brook.

SOME TRANSPORT OF BYGONE DAYS

35. The son of H. J. Fearn with one of Fearn's carriages outside their premises on Wellsic Lane. Fearn's were general carriers and the signboard on the wall lists the services they offered which included General Carriers, Furniture Removed and Open and Closed Carriages. They seem to have come late to Rothley. The business does not appear in Kelly's Directory for 1928 but does appear in the 1932 edition.

36. A horse drawn farm cart at the Cross Green end of Anthony Street. This was the face of farming right up to the beginning of WW II. The house to the left is the one shown in picture 17. The cottage behind the cart facing on to Cross Green is no longer there but it can be seen in picture 12.

35a. Today's carriers use large trucks instead of a horse and cart and the minibus has replaced the carriage. Kinch is a long established family name in Rothley and the lorry illustrated is owned by Nigel Kinch the grandson of Kenneth Kinch who established the business in Town Green Street in the 1930s.

36a. Farming was once one of the principal sources of employment in Rothley. The 1851 census lists 15 farmers and 84 agricultural labourers. There are still six farms in or close to the village but modern farming, now highly mechanised, requires far fewer workers. This large tractor and trailer, travelling along Town Green Street, is owned by the Wright's of Brookfield Farm.

37. Ken Kitching as a young man on the milk float of the Grange Dairy which used to be off Fowke Street. Ken Kitching started work at the dairy as a milk delivery boy at the age of 14 and took over the business in 1933. He originally served milk directly from churns and went on to bottling after WW II when the law changed. He was the local milkman for 41 years until he retired in 1974.

38. Cyril Chamberlain with the Co-op Society bread delivery van. He worked for the Co-op bakery in Fowke Street and eventually ran his own bakery at the shop on the corner of Howe Lane. (currently Bradley's). At one time many food retailers such as bakers, greengrocers, milkmen and so on did not have shops but delivered from vans or lorries to the door throughout the surrounding area. This delivery service is now being offered by supermarkets from whom one can order all one's groceries by computer.

37a. At the time when Ken Kitching was delivering milk to the doorstep the Co-op and Kirby & West were his main competitors. Now only Kirby & West provides the service but no-one knows for how much longer. The viability of delivery services like this are regularly called into question.

38a. The days of having bread delivered daily to the door have gone so the only reasonable contrast we can make is with the bread counter at the local supermarket from where you can have your bread delivered along with all your other groceries.

39. Bradley's in the 1930s. The business was originally based in Mountsorrel and operated by selling groceries from this van, house to house, in the surrounding area.

40. Boyer's buses outside the owner's house on Mountsorrel Lane. Harry Boyer, a carpenter, is reputed to have built the first bus in Rothley about 1911. The company grew and became one of about six plying the Leicester/Loughborough route until they were all absorbed by the Midland Red bus company. The house is currently the Limes Hotel.

39a. Bradley's today. One of their fleet of vans outside the shop in Woodgate. They opened their first shop in Quorn and established a presence in Rothley in the 1970s when they took over the shop which had previously been run by the Antill brothers and much earlier by Burnsall's the bakers.

40a. A modern bus operated by Arriva at Cross Green. The earlier Midland Red buses enjoyed a monopoly for a number of years but bus companies were deregulated in the 1980s and we are once again served by several companies who cover a network of routes throughout the area.

41. The hazards of travelling by public transport in the 1930s. A bus in collision with what is almost certainly the parapet of Nott bridge on Hallfields Lane (see picture 5). It must have been incidents like this which finally necessitated the remodelling and widening of the bridge.

42. A Kemp & Shaw bus stranded on Hallfields Lane in the floods of 1932. The low parapet to the left is believed to belong to a culvert which carried water under the road from Bunney's field where a ditch runs along the Anthony Street side. These floods were widespread and Ashby de la Zouch was so badly affected that the Leicester Mercury started a relief fund.

41a. A modern bus crossing the bridge on Hallfields Lane has no such problems as that on the opposite page.

42a. This view is taken close to where the Kemp & Shaw bus was stranded in 1932. It demonstrates the flood defences in operation today and shows the efficiency of the flood bank on the right. Before it was built and with the water level as high as this all the land to the right which is flanked by Town Green Street would have been flooded.

THE HUMAN SIDE OF ROTHLEY HISTORY

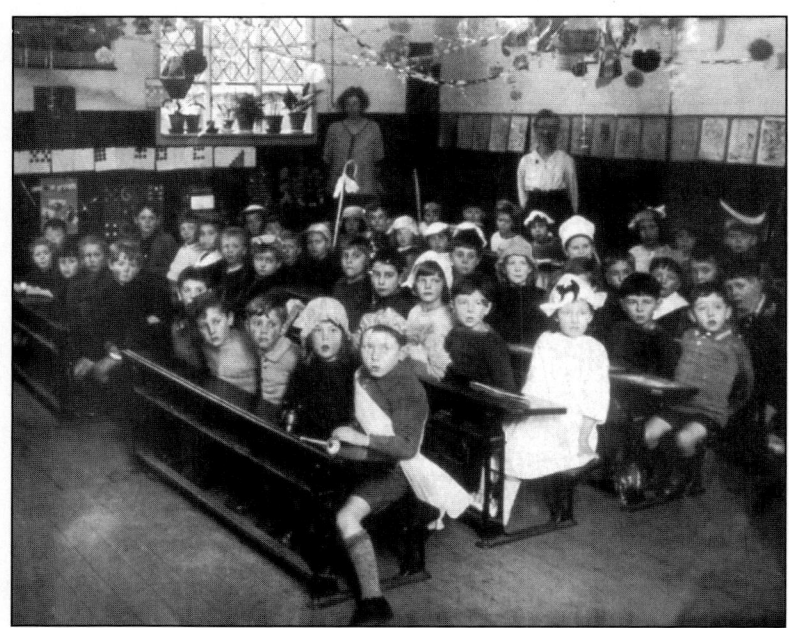

43. Rothley Junior school in the 1920s at the old school in School Street. The two teachers at the rear of the class are Miss Haywood, the headmistress, on the right and Miss Hands, who apparently cycled from Leicester each day. The National School owes its origin to the Rev. William Ackworth in 1837. In 1870 primary education became compulsory so in 1871 the Rev. Richard Burton organised the purchase of cottages next to the school, to which he made a considerable donation, so that it could be enlarged to accommodate the increased number of pupils.

44. Rev. Richard Burton came to Rothley as curate in 1856 and became vicar in 1869: a post he held until his death in 1909. He was an extremely influential member of the local community. Among other things he was responsible for the restoration of the church in 1877 (see picture 44a). He also played a major part in the life of the village, serving as a JP and as Chairman of the first civil Parish Council.

43a. A modern classroom in the Church of England school on Mountsorrel Lane. By 1901 more space was required to accommodate increasing numbers of children and in 1902 the infants moved to new premises (built by Sleath & Son) in Mountsorrel Lane. After an extension in 1913 the juniors moved to Mountsorrel Lane and the infants returned to School Street. Further expansion in 1968 finally provided accommodation for both groups on the one site. The school remains there to this day and has been much extended since.

44a. This watercolour painting, dated 1897, shows the interior of the church not long after its restoration. The most noticeable feature, removed about 1970, is the large cross that was installed above the chancel screen. According to a report at the time of the restoration the walls and roof were on the point of collapse. As well as repairing the fabric the wooden porch on the south side was replaced by the stone built entrance on the north side, the chancel was extended and the vestry and organ chamber were added. The church we have today is a lasting memorial to the Rev. Richard Burton.

The painting is the work of Robert Jackson Emerson, born in North Street in Rothley in 1878, who became an artist and sculptor of note. He was an inspired teacher and spent most of his career at the Wolverhampton School of Art.

45. Frank Sleath. F. Sleath & Son became the most important builders in Rothley. The company was responsible for building many of the brick terraces and cottages erected around the turn of the 20th century and up to World War I. They can be found in North Street, Anthony Street, Woodgate, Howe Lane and Mountsorrel Lane and are generally distinguishable by the carved stone name tablets with date set into the frontages. They typically sold for about £150 when they were built.

46. Mrs. Cecilia Draper (left) and her daughter Mrs. Muriel Calloway. Mrs. Draper ran the Rothley telephone exchange from 1914 to 1946. First in North Street and subsequently in the front room of 72 Woodgate. In the other picture, Mrs. Calloway is seen at the switchboard in Woodgate. At a time when one could only be connected via the operator it meant that the girls on the switchboard were privy to much of the gossip that went on in the village.

45a. The inscribed and carved stone plaque on the front of the memorial cottages on North Street. F. Sleath & Son were responsible for considerable changes to the appearance of the village, giving it much of the character it has today. They replaced a number of timbered and thatched cottages with what were then modern buildings as well as building on new sites.

46a. The present automatic telephone exchange is opposite the site of the earlier manual one in Woodgate. It may be more efficient and functional but it lacks the personal touch that was an integral part of dialling the operator to request a number. The exchange was once called Rothley Park.

47. Benjamin Armstrong (1813-1904) claimed to be the last framework knitter in Rothley. He must have been a very well-known character in Rothley since he had a small workshop in Bacon Hole, off Town Green Street, which became known as Armstrong's Yard. During the 19th century framework knitting of stockings was one of the major occupations in Rothley. In the 1851 census 132 people were recorded as framework knitters but by 1891 only 12 were listed.

48. This engraving of a stocking frame was published in 1751. The machine had changed little by the time Armstrong was working on one installed in his workshop in Bacon Hole in the late 19th century. Similar machines can still be seen in the Framework Knitter's Museum at Wigston near Leicester and at Ruddington near Nottingham.

47a. The introduction of the more compact circular knitting machine in the late 19th century quickly replaced the cumbersome knitting frame. Easily connected to mechanical power the hosiery factory arrived and the days of knitting as a cottage industry were over. The first such factory in Rothley was Victoria Mills in Fowke Street built by Harry Hames and opened in 1887. It probably looked similar to this photo of an unknown hosiery factory taken about 1900. Victoria Mills today houses a variety of companies engaged in a range of light industries including electronics, spectacles and talking books.

48a. The knitting frame was also mechanised with the introduction of the Cotton's Patent Hosiery Machine shown here. This one, of 1893, could knit six stockings at once.

49. The Hickling brothers in the Woodman's Stroke? Undated but probably in the early years of the 20th century. The two men appear to be of similar ages.
In 1881 Edward Hickling (57) was listed only as a wheelwright although he was living in Church Street and James was apparently not recorded. The 1891 census lists Edward as wheelwright and licensee and James as a tailor, living with his sister Mary in Cross green. Other Hicklings are listed but they are all too young to be either of the men above.

50. Rothley's football team was known as the Swifts when this picture was taken in 1897. Unfortunately we have no names for the players.

49a. The Woodman's Stroke today. It appears to have been commonplace for innkeepers to have an additional occupation; usually farming. The Hicklings were also undertakers and the village bier was apparently kept at the pub. Perhaps the income from keeping an inn was neither profitable enough nor time consuming enough to provide an adequate living?

50a. Rothley's sporting tradition continues today with the Rothley Imps football team. Left to right; *back row,* A. Lee (Joint manager), A. Capell, N. Skinner, H. White, T. Kee (Joint manager), R. Sutherington, S. Kilby, R. Stone, T. Slack, R. Bulmer, J. McPhee; *front row* J. Warner, D. Partner, S. Kee, M. Schultz, B. Ashdown, G. Ottewell.

SOME THINGS CHANGE MORE SLOWLY

51. The Ridings looking towards Rothley Court Hotel. This view, on the down slope between the Ridgeway and Westfield Lane must be one of the least changed in Rothley. The stamp on the postcard from which this view is taken was cancelled '5 APR 23'.

52. Rothley Station as it was. The Manchester, Sheffield & Lincoln Railway was the last major railway to be built but it had changed its name to the Great Central Railway by the time it arrived in Rothley in 1899. It became a major factor in the development of Rothley as a residential suburb of Leicester and it is said that some local businessmen travelled by train four times a day, coming home from Leicester for lunch. The line became the London North Eastern Railway in 1922 and was nationalised in 1947.

51a. A winter view of the Ridings taken from the same viewpoint as picture 51 but little has changed. The tree on the extreme left could be the same tree seen there. The only horses seen today are those ridden for pleasure and there is now a proper footpath on the right side.

52a. Rothley Station today. This is another view that can have changed little since the heyday of steam railways. The station closed in 1963, as part of the Beeching plan, but it has since been re-opened by the Great Central Railway Steam Trust which has set out to recreate the age of steam travel. It now attracts visitors from all over the country. There have been few changes other than to the signal box which has been moved from the other side of the site.

BIBLIOGRAPHY

The following list contains details of the books and papers relating to Rothley and its history of which we are aware. If the reader knows of any others the History Society would be pleased to hear of them. Most of the publications listed are not readily available but copies may generally be found in the Family History section of Loughborough Public Library, Granby Street, Loughborough or the Leicestershire County Record Office, Long Street, Wigston Magna which also stores many other documents relating to Rothley.

Author	Title	Date	Notes
J. Nicholls	The History & Antiquities of the County of Leicester	1804	The classic work on Leicestershire that includes the early recorded history of Rothley.
Leicester Archaeological Society	History of Rothley	1921	A series of papers by specialist historians on the Temple, the Manor and the Church.
R. Packe	Rothley	1958	A personal view of the history of Rothley by a longtime resident.
P. Britt	Rothley School 1871-1992	2ndEd. 1991	
T. Sheppard	The Peculiar Parish	1994	A topographical survey of the parish.
W.E.A.	Rothley in 1851	1994	An analysis of the 1851 census return relating to Rothley.
P. Britt	Victorian Rothley	1995	A Glimpse of Village Life.
T. Sheppard	The National School in Rothley	1996	A history of the Church of England School in Rothley.
T. Sheppard	Patronage Anchored	1998	The history of the living of the Church of St. Mary and St. John.
T. Sheppard	Rothley Sources	1999	This records all the references to Rothley known to the author and will save hours for anyone wishing to do their own research.
C.M. Wessel	The Knights Hospitaller of St. John	1999	This is a short history of the Knights Templar and Hospitaller in Leicestershire generally, including Rothley.